MONEY SMART

SPENDING

Dennis Brindell Fradin & Judith Bloom Fradin

MONEY SMART

SPENDING

Dennis Brindell Fradin & Judith Bloom Fradin

Marshall Cavendish
Benchmark
New York

Other Marshall Cavendish Offices:
Marshall Cavendish International (Asia) Private Limited, 1 New Industrial Road, Singapore 536196 • Marshall Cavendish International (Thailand) Co Ltd. 253 Asoke, 12th Flr, Sukhumvit 21 Road, Klongtoey Nua, Wattana, Bangkok 10110, Thailand • Marshall Cavendish (Malaysia) Sdn Bhd, Times Subang, Lot 46, Subang Hi-Tech Industrial Park, Batu Tiga, 40000 Shah Alam, Selangor Darul Ehsan, Malaysia

Marshall Cavendish is a trademark of Times Publishing Limited

All websites were available and accurate when this book was sent to press.

Library of Congress Cataloging-in-Publication Data
Fradin, Dennis B.
Spending / by Dennis Brindell Fradin & Judith Bloom Fradin.
p. cm. — (Money smart)
Includes bibliographical references and index.
Summary: "Answers basic questions students ask when learning about spending money and other financial skills needed for adulthood: strategies for making a budget; spending with cash versus credit; and whether to rent or buy a place to live"—Provided by publisher.
ISBN 978-1-60870-126-1
1. Finance, Personal—Juvenile literature. 2. Money—Juvenile literature.
I. Fradin, Judith Bloom. II. Title.
HG179.F687 2010
332.024—dc22
2009050435

Editor: Deborah Grahame
Publisher: Michelle Bisson
Art Director: Anahid Hamparian
Series Designer: Kay Petronio
Photo research by Connie Gardner

Cover photo by Erik Dreyer/Getty Images

The photographs in this book are used by permission and through the courtesy of: *Art Archive;* National Anthropological Museum/Mexico/Gianni Dagli Orti, 6; *Granger Collection:* 9; *Getty Images:* Dana Neely, 13; Paul Venning, 14; Joe Raedie, 27; Don Klumpp, 29; Stephen Marks, 30; Bruce Ayers, 32; Digital Vision, 41; David Bloomer, 45; Yellow Dog Productions, 46; Emmanuel Faure, 50; Jeff Cadge, 55;*The Image Works:* Jeff Greenberg, 18; David Grossman, 23; Bob Daemmrich, 35; Jim West, 42; *Corbis:* Luis Pelaez, 16; Alan Schein, 20.

Printed in Malaysia (T)

135642

CONTENTS

Scientists believe that hunters crossed the Bering Strait, a then-frozen body of water separating Asia from North America, more than 25,000 years ago. They may have come in search of food during the last Ice Age.

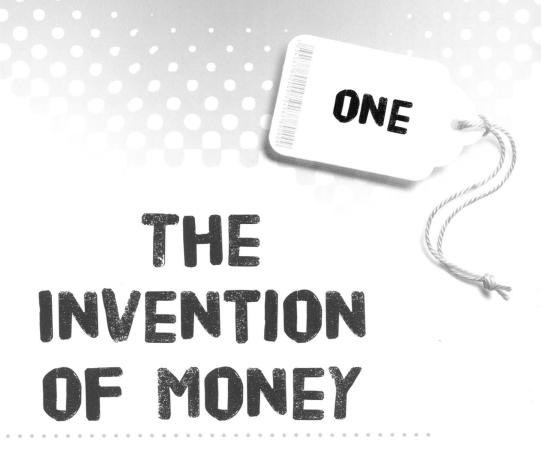

ONE

THE INVENTION OF MONEY

Many thousands of years ago, there was no money. People traded with one another for what they needed. For example, a family with a cow might trade milk for eggs from another family. A woman who sewed might trade clothing for bread from a farmer. An injured hunter might pay a healer with a slab of meat.

People in the kingdom of Lydia, in what is now the country of Turkey, created the first coins more than 2,600 years ago. The Chinese first issued paper money between 1,400 and 2,000 years ago. Over the centuries, other countries also produced coins and paper currency so their people could pay for goods.

In the 1600s and early 1700s, England established thirteen colonies in North America. Some of the colonies issued their own money. Massachusetts issued coins called willow tree pieces and pine tree pieces, while Maryland created Lord Baltimore shillings. There was no single, well-developed monetary system for all thirteen colonies. The American colonists mostly used money from other countries, including pesos ("pieces of eight") from Spain, guilders from the Netherlands, and pounds from England.

The thirteen colonies declared their independence from England in 1776. American leaders decided that their new country, the United States of America, needed a monetary system. In 1792 the United States adopted its own unit of money, the dollar. The word *dollar* derives from *thaler*, which was a type of coin first made in Bohemia (the present-day Czech Republic). Americans have used dollars as their basic unit of currency for about 220 years.

Each of the world's countries has a monetary unit. Some countries share a monetary unit. For example, France, Greece, Ireland, Portugal,

The pine tree coin, minted in Massachusetts between 1667 and 1674, was one of the earliest American coins.

DEBT IN THE GOOD OLD DAYS

It was much worse to fall into debt in early America than it is today. In the 1700s, people who owed large sums of money were thrown into debtors' prisons. Robert Morris was one sad case. Nicknamed the Financier of the Revolution, Morris spent his own money on food, supplies, and salaries for American soldiers. He signed both the Declaration of Independence and the U.S. Constitution. Yet because he fell into debt, he later spent three and a half years in the Philadelphia debtors' prison known as Prune Street.

"BENJAMINS" & OTHER U.S. MONEY

Over the centuries, people around the world have used some odd objects as money. The people of the Yap Islands in the Pacific Ocean used large stones as money. Some of their stone money was up to 12 feet (3.5 meters) in diameter and weighed hundreds or even thousands of pounds (kilograms). People used blocks of tea as money in China, Tibet, and Siberia, while Ethiopians used blocks of salt. Some American Indian money was made of shell beads called wampum. In the colony of Virginia, people used tobacco to pay taxes, salaries, fines, and debts.

and more than a dozen other European nations share a currency called the euro. In Japan the basic unit of money is the yen, and in China it is the yuan. Russians pay their bills with rubles, South Africans with rands, Icelanders with kronas, Kenyans with shillings, Israelis with shekels, and Guatemalans with quetzals. Several nations outside the United States use the U.S. dollar as their official currency.

Regardless of what their currency is called, people around the world share one complaint. In thousands of languages they say, "Everything costs too much!"

A nurse documents patient information. Many jobs are available in health care, and it is expected that many more will be created.

TWO

WHY DO PEOPLE WORK?

Until the 1960s, most men in the United States had jobs. Few women worked outside the home. Times have changed. In 2010, three out of every four American women held jobs outside the home. In most households at least two family members worked—usually the husband and the wife.

A typical American worker puts in an eight-hour workday for five days a week, fifty weeks a year. That amounts to two thousand hours of work per year. Some people put in more hours than that. They work extra-long days and even weekends. Other people have two or more jobs. For instance, during the evenings, a teacher might tutor kids who need help with their schoolwork. A car mechanic might work as a hotel desk clerk on Saturdays and Sundays. A struggling actor, writer, or artist might have a day job waiting tables.

Why do people work so hard? Some people love what they do and find it difficult to tear themselves away from their work. The main reason, though, is that people need money.

The weary student or job-seeker is a familiar sight in libraries and coffee shops.

JOB OR CAREER?

A career is the kind of work a person does, such as nursing or education. A job is the specific title for the work that a person does.

In 2010, the median (average) household income in the United States was a little over $50,000 a year. In other words, the typical American family earned a little over $50,000 from their salaries and other types of income. That may sound like a lot of money, yet many families spend all, or nearly all, of their income. Some families spend *more* than they earn, which means that they are in debt—a situation that can cause serious financial trouble. In the next three chapters, we will look at the goods and services on which people spend their hard-earned money.

Young families need to be aware of their spending habits by reviewing each month's bills and financial statements.

"BEWARE OF LITTLE EXPENSES"

In his 1758 essay "The Way to Wealth," Benjamin Franklin writes, "Beware of little expenses; a small leak will sink a great ship." More than 250 years later, Franklin's advice still rings true. The typical American family spends money on dozens of what Franklin might call "little expenses" each week.

For example, taking your dog for a visit to the groomer can cost $40. The same is true for a private ballet lesson for a child. A haircut costs around $15 for a child, $20 for a man, and $40 for a woman.

A simple haircut is one of life's little necessities, but it's possible to overspend on hair care to the point that it becomes a luxury.

Parking a car all day in a downtown lot can cost $50 in some major cities. A first-class stamp costs 44 cents. Although this may not seem like much, it adds up to $22 if you mail fifty holiday greeting cards. Similarly, a late fee of 15 cents a day per library book doesn't sound expensive, but months of overdue books can cost you a good deal of money. For example, an author we'll call Dennis recently paid a $15 fine for overdue books, and he is ashamed to say that his record is about $50. You can buy a baseball bat—or get your car washed five times—for $50.

Be prepared to hand over a $20 bill for a pizza delivered to your door, and you'll need $1.50 for a bottled soft drink at a convenience store. While a dollar and a half won't ruin anyone's finances, consider this: if you spend that much on an energy drink or a bag of chips every day, over the course of a year it will add up to $547.50.

In some cases, people spend money to support their bad habits. Millions of people around the country play lotteries. A woman we'll call Cecilia buys $20 in lottery tickets each week. At that rate, Cecilia spends more than a thousand dollars on the lottery every year.

Speaking of bad habits, as of 2010, a pack of cigarettes cost $9 in some places in the United States. A smoker who buys a pack a day spends about $3,300 on cigarettes in one year. Besides putting a dent in the smoker's pocketbook, this habit is damaging his or her health.

In all, most families spend a few thousand dollars a year on little expenses, which are also called miscellaneous expenses. As you will soon see, people spend even more on certain big-ticket items.

High-rise apartments are convenient for people living in large cities.

HOUSING: THE NUMBER-ONE EXPENSE

For most people, the largest single expense is paying for a place to live. There are two basic kinds of housing. Roughly one-third of all Americans rent apartments. About two-thirds buy entire homes.

Apartment dwellers pay rent to a landlord—the owner of the building. The rent may be anywhere from a few hundred to many thousands of dollars per month. The apartment's size is a major factor in determining the amount of the rent. For example, a three-bedroom apartment generally has a higher rent than a one-bedroom apartment. Another key factor is location. An apartment in what is considered a safe, upscale neighborhood with trendy stores and fancy restaurants usually costs more than an apartment in a neighborhood with decaying buildings and a high crime rate.

Rents vary from city to city. As of 2010, the average rent for an apartment in Los Angeles, California, or Chicago, Illinois, was a whopping $2,000 per month. Apartments in New York City rented for an average of $1,600 a month. Renters were paying an average of about $1,000 per month in Savannah, Georgia, and Santa Fe, New Mexico, and an average of $700 per month in Austin, Texas, Denver, Colorado, and Phoenix, Arizona.

Apartment living has several advantages. For one thing, apartment dwellers don't have the headache of maintaining the building. If the roof springs a leak, the heat breaks down, or the water pipes burst, the tenants (another word for renters) don't have to spend thousands of dollars for repairs. That is the landlord's responsibility. Unlike home owners, renters usually don't have to mow the lawn, shovel snow, pay property taxes, or worry about selling the property if they decide to move. In addition, their rent often includes the costs of heat and water.

People now pay top dollar to live in these upscale Brooklyn brownstones, considered standard housing in the nineteenth century.

Renting also has drawbacks. You might have noisy neighbors upstairs or across the hall. It can be expensive and time-consuming to park in crowded public areas or on the street. The biggest disadvantage is that tenants spend a lot of money on housing, but they do not end up owning anything. Imagine a family that pays $2,000 a month for an apartment that they live in for a decade. That amounts to $240,000 over those ten years. The family has a place to live, yet at the end of the ten years they do not own even a brick in their building.

Home buyers, on the other hand, invest in a dwelling that becomes theirs. In 2010, the average new home in the United States cost about $250,000. As with apartments, the size and location of the house largely determine its selling price. A huge home in a ritzy suburb can sell for millions of dollars, while a small house in a town with a falling population might sell for just several thousand dollars.

MOVING ON UP

If you sell your house, you get to keep all the money except what you owe the bank. Many people use the money they make selling one house as their down payment for a larger house.

Few people can afford to pay for an entire house at once, especially if the home is pricey. What do prospective home buyers do if they don't have the entire sum? Most take out a mortgage. A home mortgage is a large loan provided by a bank or other financial institution.

To illustrate how a mortgage works, let's look at the experience of a fictitious couple, Ernie and Rosalie Washington. Ernie and Rosalie, who have a daughter and a son, find a house they like in a suburb known for its good schools and friendly neighbors. The home they want costs $200,000, however, and Ernie and Rosalie have saved only $50,000. That $50,000 becomes their down payment—money they pay when they first purchase the house. They go to a bank and borrow the remaining $150,000 that they need to complete the purchase. This big bank loan is their mortgage.

A home buyer usually repays his or her mortgage in monthly installments over many years. The Washingtons arrange to repay their loan over thirty years—a typical length of time. Banks do not provide mortgage money out of the goodness of their hearts. For the privilege of borrowing money from a bank, home buyers must not only repay the loan, but also add an extra amount of money known as interest. The interest rate on the Washingtons' $150,000 mortgage is 6 percent. This means that they must pay the bank about $900 every month for thirty years. Once the Washingtons make their last payment, they will own the house completely.

Taking out a mortgage is extremely expensive. A $900 monthly mortgage payment over thirty years amounts to $900 x 12 x 30, or

$324,000. For the privilege of borrowing $150,000, the Washingtons will pay about $175,000 in interest alone.

Now, imagine that Rosalie loses her job, and the Washingtons can no longer afford to make their monthly mortgage payment. The bank can then start a foreclosure—a process that can result in the bank taking over a house and forcing the occupants to leave. This may seem harsh, but banks are in the business of making money. They can't lend a couple $150,000 and not get their money back along with the interest.

During hard times, when many people lose their jobs and can't make their mortgage payments, home foreclosures can become a national catastrophe. For example, during the recession that began in late 2007, the unemployment rate rose to just over 10 percent by October 2009—the highest jobless rate in the United States in more than twenty-five years. One result was that many families could not pay their mortgages. Between August 2007 and mid-2009, about 1.5 million American families—totaling about 6 million people—lost their homes due to foreclosures.

Besides being a terrible experience, getting forced out of a foreclosed home can be very costly. In addition to losing their residence, the family loses all the money they have put into it up to that point.

Most families are able to continue making mortgage payments

During the U.S. housing crisis, millions of homeowners owed their lenders more than they could pay and faced foreclosure as a result.

even in hard times. However, homes have other ways of ruining a family's finances. Imagine this: During a rainstorm you hear a drip-drip-drip, and suddenly a puddle forms in your living room. You need a new $10,000 roof. A major problem develops in your underground water pipes. There goes a few thousand dollars to the plumber. Then, because your retired grandparents are moving in,

RECESSION AND DEPRESSION

A recession occurs when business activity slumps. Many people lose their jobs and homes, and some businesses go bankrupt. A recent example is the recession starting in 2007. If a recession gets bad enough, it becomes what economists call a depression. The Great Depression of 1929 to 1939 was the worst depression in our country's history. By 1933, one-quarter of all workers were jobless—two and a half times the jobless rate in 2009.

you need to build an addition on your home. The cost of building the addition may top $50,000.

Despite the expenses, many people feel that the pluses of home ownership outweigh the negatives. A house offers privacy that apartments often lack. You can decorate your house the way you please. You might have a yard where you can socialize with your friends, enjoy a barbecue, and grow a flower or vegetable garden. You can have a dog if you want. And as you continue to pay off your mortgage, a larger and larger percentage of the house becomes yours.

Even though applying for a mortgage involves much paperwork and can be stressful, the transition to home ownership is a happy one.

Some people prepare their own taxes when doing yearly tax returns, while others use accountants or tax professionals.

OTHER BIG-TICKET ITEMS

FIVE

Taxes are another major expense for most people. In fact, the typical American family spends about one-third of its total income on various types of taxes each year.

Federal income tax takes the largest bite out of a family's income. Not counting people who don't earn enough money to be taxed, every American with an income is expected to pay taxes to the Internal Revenue Service (IRS). In simple terms, here is how Americans calculate the taxes they owe "Uncle Sam," or the United States government.

THE ORIGIN OF "UNCLE SAM"

Many Americans refer to the U.S. government as "Uncle Sam." During the War of 1812, a man named Sam Wilson opened a meatpacking plant in Troy, New York. Meat that Wilson shipped to the army was stamped "U.S." This stood for "United States." However, the workers in the meatpacking plant joked that the letters stood for Uncle Sam, which is what they called Wilson. By 1815, Uncle Sam had caught on as a nickname for the U.S. government.

First, you add up your income from wages, tips (extra pay service workers earn from customers), interest, and other money you received over the course of the year. Then you subtract home mortgage interest, expenses relating to your job, and other items that the government allows you to deduct from your total income. The result is called your taxable income. Then you look on a chart to see how much tax you owe Uncle Sam for the year.

For example, Ernie and Rosalie Washington had a taxable income of $70,000 in 2008. According to the tax chart, this means they owe $10,194 in taxes for that year. Generally, the higher a family's income, the more they owe the IRS. Had the Washingtons earned $60,000 in 2008, their taxes would have amounted to $8,201.

Most Americans do not pay their federal taxes all at once. Instead, they pay the money gradually. In most cases, a portion of the tax money is taken off each of a worker's paychecks. The money pays for federal highways and buildings, the salaries of U.S. lawmakers, the U.S. Armed Forces, the space program, and other programs supported by federal tax dollars.

Additional federal taxes include Social Security and Medicare. Social Security provides income for elderly and retired people and their families. Medicare provides health insurance for men and women aged sixty-five or older and for disabled people of all ages.

WHAT IS INSURANCE?

Now and then people have automobile accidents that cause injuries and wreck cars. Occasionally homes go up in flames or are damaged by falling trees. Sometimes people enter hospitals to be treated for illnesses. Insurance helps pay for these events. A client pays a fee called a premium to an insurance company. In return, the company pays part (or all) of the costs if disaster strikes. Common types of insurance include automobile, homeowners, health, and life insurance. Insurance companies make money because the kinds of events they cover don't happen very often.

In addition to federal taxes, the residents of most states are also required to pay state income taxes. That money pays for schools, state highways, and other services. Americans also pay property taxes, as well as various other local, state, and federal taxes. Add it all together, and the typical American family pays nearly $20,000 a year in taxes.

Transportation has become very costly—especially in today's economy, when a tankful of gasoline can cost $50. The typical American family spends about $10,000 a year just getting where they want to go. Much of this money goes toward the purchase and upkeep of an automobile, including fuel. Families that travel by public transportation, such as buses and trains, generally spend less than $10,000 a year to get around.

In colonial America, nearly everyone did at least some farming. Because families grew their own food crops and raised their own livestock, their food costs were minimal. Today fewer Americans are farmers, which means that most people buy their food at the grocery store. People who don't regularly shop for food are often shocked by its high cost. For example, in 2010, skirt steak cost about $5 a pound, as did boneless turkey breast. A dozen eggs cost $3—about the same as a bag of salad or 8 ounces of American cheese. Salmon fillets were $10 a pound, and a 12-inch cake cost

The average retail price for a gallon of gas is dictated by the price per barrel of crude oil, set months before the fuel reaches the pumps.

around $9. In all, the typical American family spends about $2,500 per person for food annually. With a growing daughter and son, Ernie and Rosalie spent about $10,000 per year on food during the early 2000s.

Health care is another big expense for millions of families. Some American employers pay for all or part of their employees' health insurance. Self-employed people must pay for all of their health insurance themselves, however. And many families have no health insurance at all because they can't afford it. As a result, when someone gets sick and needs to be hospitalized, different families pay anywhere from nothing at all to tens of thousands of dollars.

Utilities are another big-ticket item. Utilities include electricity, heating, water, telephone, cable TV, and computer service. On average, U.S. households spend $3,000 to $4,000 per year on utilities.

There are many other expenses. Some families spend a few thousand dollars per year on vacations and entertainment. The typical family of four spends $2,000 to $3,000 per year on clothing and shoes. Furniture, diapers, and clothing for a baby's first year can easily cost $1,000.

For a few years, at least, many families have one more giant expense. More than half of all Americans attend college. Tuition at a

COLLEGE=KNOWLEDGE+MONEY

Higher education provides a person with not only knowledge, but also a larger income. Over the course of their lives, people with college degrees earn about twice the money as people with only a high school diploma.

state school can run $12,000 a year, which adds up to $48,000 for a four-year education. A private college or university can cost $40,000 a year, or $160,000 for four years. And the annual cost of college is much higher, considering that students need to pay for books and additional expenses.

Filling out a deposit slip at a bank. As society goes paperless, online banking and sales transactions are becoming more common.

SIX

HOW PEOPLE PAY FOR THINGS

There are several ways to pay for goods and services. Most people have a checking account at a bank. They deposit their paychecks and other income into their bank account. They might mail checks to the bank or take money in personally to make a deposit. In a process known as direct deposit, many people have their paychecks sent electronically to their bank.

Let's say you have $2,000 in your checking account. You can write checks totaling $2,000, but no more than that. Paying a bill by check is easy—it's just a matter of filling in the blanks. You fill in the date on the check and the name of the person or business receiving the money. Then you write out the amount of the check—both in numbers and in words so that it is perfectly clear how much money you intend to pay. Finally, you sign the check.

You also keep a record of the check—and of how much money remains in your account—in a booklet called a checkbook. For example, if you begin a week with $2,000 in your checking account, and during the course of the week you write checks for $1,000, $50, and $175, then you will have a balance of $775.

You must be careful with your math to keep a bank account running smoothly. Because of mathematical mistakes, people sometimes write checks for more money than they have in their bank accounts. Suppose you think you have $3,000 in your account, when you actually have only $2,000, and you write a check for $2,500. In that case the recipient can't cash your check because you don't have enough money to cover it. When you write a check for more money than you have in your account, banks call it an overdraft. This is also called bouncing a check. Banks charge fees for bouncing checks, so you should always avoid it.

Some people prefer to pay cash—actual bills and coins—for certain purchases. For example, if a husband buys a present for his wife and the couple shares a credit card account, he might want to pay cash so

Some people use "cold, hard cash" instead of credit or debit cards to keep better control over their spending.

she won't know how much he spent on the gift. Another reason some people prefer to spend cash is that they want to avoid paying bank fees for writing checks.

One way to obtain cash is to write yourself a check at the bank. Another way is to get cash from an automatic teller machine (ATM). First, you insert an ATM card into the machine. You then type in a secret code number, known as your personal identification number or PIN, on the ATM keyboard. This secret number prevents other people from stealing money out of your account. After you enter your PIN, you enter the amount of money you want. The machine makes coughing noises for a few seconds before spitting out your money, along with a receipt for your transaction.

Of course the ATM doesn't *give* you the money as a present. The money is taken out of your bank account, along with a small fee in some cases. You must remember to subtract the amount of the ATM

The first ATM was installed in Enfield, England, in 1967. The networked ATM was developed by a Texas engineer in 1968.

transaction in your checkbook. A big reason for bouncing checks is that people forget to write down ATM withdrawals. Then they have less money in their accounts than they think.

You may have heard a cashier at a store ask a customer, "Credit or debit?" A debit card is another way to pay for purchases. With a debit card, the money is taken directly out of your bank account. Let's say you have $750 in your checking account. You go to the store and buy $223.35 worth of groceries. You pay the bill with a swipe of your debit card. You then have $526.65 left in your account. Usually the same card can be used as both an ATM card and a debit card.

Last but definitely not least, Americans pay for goods and services with credit cards—lots and lots of credit cards. As of 2009, there were more than a billion credit cards in Americans' wallets and purses—an average of about five per adult. Three-quarters of all U.S. households have at least one credit card. Credit cards are issued by banks, stores, and oil and phone companies. People can use them to pay for nearly everything, from airplane flights to zoo tickets.

Credit cards, also called "plastic," are convenient and easy to use. If you have a credit card, you don't have to walk around with a lot of cash or write a check and show identification with every purchase. Just swipe the plastic, and then pay for all your credit card purchases at once when your monthly bill is due.

CREDIT CARD CHARGES ARE A LOAN

Many people mistakenly think of a credit card as money in their pockets. When you buy something using plastic, you are actually borrowing money from the credit card company. If you don't repay all the money when it's due, you have to pay steep interest on this loan.

Plastic can also have pitfalls. For one thing, credit cards make it so easy to spend money that they can lure people into buying items they really can't afford. Financial expert and author Michelle Singletary calls this phenomenon "CCC (credit card craziness)." Others call it "overspenditis." Do you see a video game or a camera that you kind of want but don't really need? With a swipe of your credit card, it's yours. Plastic takes care of it, and you can worry about the bill later.

For households that pay their bills on time, using credit cards makes life simpler. The problem is, most people *don't* pay their total credit card balances on time. As of 2010, the average credit card debt for families with one or more cards was a staggering $11,000. This debt can increase month after month, especially because credit card companies charge interest on unpaid bills. In fact, credit card companies make most of their money by charging interest, so they actually prefer that people *not* pay all that they owe when their credit card bills come due.

Millions of Americans will require years and even decades to pay off their credit card debts—if they ever do. In the next chapter we will look at a way people can better manage their money.

Credit cards are a convenience at the mall, but can lead to inconvenient interest and late fees if you carry a balance or miss a payment.

Families can consult financial websites prior to deciding how to spend and save their money.

SEVEN

MAKING A BUDGET

Family A's income is $120,000 a year. Family B's is $60,000. Which family is better off financially? At first glance, this seems like an easy question. With twice as much income, Family A appears to be doing better. But wait a moment! To answer the question, we must first know how much each household spends. What if Family A spends $125,000 a year, but Family B spends only $55,000? Then Family B would be in better shape because they are saving $5,000 a year, while Family A is digging themselves into a financial hole by spending $5,000 more than they earn. Unless they change their ways, Family A could lose their home and other possessions.

Here is a cardinal rule of handling money: don't spend more than you earn. That's easier said than done! With mortgage payments, taxes, utilities, clothing, medical bills, insurance, and many more expenses, how can a family with a medium income get by? One technique is to make a budget—a plan for spending.

With a budget, you assign a certain amount of money for each type of expense, and you make sure that the total doesn't exceed your household income. A budget is like a coach's game plan or an author's outline for a book. For a budget to work, however, a family has to stick to it, which means that it must be realistic.

Imagine that Ernie and Rosalie Washington are making a budget for the year 2011. After taxes, their income should be around $60,000. This means that their budget should allow them to spend up to $60,000. If they can spend less than that, fine, but if they spend more, they may soon face financial trouble. Budgeting isn't easy for Ernie and Rosalie; they have a new home, and their daughter Stephanie is in college. Here is their spending plan for the year 2011:

2011 BUDGET FOR WASHINGTON FAMILY (EXPECTED INCOME = $60,000 AFTER TAXES)

Expense	Amount Budgeted for 2011
House Mortgage Payments	$11,000
Food for Four People	$8,500
Transportation	$8,000
Insurance	$6,000
Medical & Dental Care	$3,000
Utilities	$3,500
Vacation & Entertainment	$2,000
Clothing	$2,000
College	$6,000
Miscellaneous	$4,000
Emergency & Unexpected Costs	$2,000
Total	$56,000
Money Left for Savings	$4,000

You may have noticed that something seems wrong about the Washington family's budget. The average American family pays $10,000 a year on transportation. How can the Washingtons spend only $8,000? A four-person family's annual food bill is typically $10,000, yet the Washingtons budgeted just $8,500. Clothing costs a family of four about $2,500, yet Ernie and Rosalie plan to spend only $2,000. What about college costs? How can the Washingtons budget only $6,000 a year for their daughter's college education when a state school costs $12,000 a year and a private college costs more than $30,000? We will solve these mysteries in the final chapter.

Shopping for bargains is one way to hang out with friends. Another way is getting together for a clothing swap to trade items you don't wear anymore.

HOW TO PAY LESS AND SPEND WISELY

Some people know how to live within their means, while others always seem to be in debt no matter how much money they earn. Here are a few financial tips on how to spend less money and live within a budget. Nearly all of these suggestions come from the books listed in the Bibliography.

HOUSING

If there is one thing to remember about housing, it is this: millions of families have been swallowed by financial quicksand because they bought homes or rented apartments they couldn't afford. It is wiser to live in a modest dwelling that you can readily pay for rather than one that stretches the family budget to the breaking point. By today's standards, the Washington family's $200,000 home qualifies as modest.

FOOD

There are ways to spend less money on food without resorting to eating ramen noodles and boxed macaroni and cheese all the time. For example, in newspapers and on the Web, you can find coupons that offer reduced prices for groceries. These coupons can save a shopper hundreds of dollars over the course of a year. Buying groceries when they are on sale can further lower food costs. Yet another way to spend less money while eating delicious fresh food is to grow a vegetable garden. Using these methods, the Washingtons expect to save $1,500 on their yearly food expenses.

TRANSPORTATION

How do the Washingtons expect to save $2,000 on transportation costs? Instead of buying a new car, they plan to purchase a cheaper, used vehicle. They have also found a cheaper and healthier way than driving to make short trips. They ride their bicycles, which saves gasoline and provides them with exercise.

INSURANCE

For many people, the biggest insurance bill is not for their car or home, but for their medical coverage. Health insurance costs have skyrocketed in recent years. As a result, millions of Americans have changed careers just to find a job that pays for their health insurance. Rosalie Washington found a new teaching job in a school district that offers better health insurance for her family than her old job did.

MEDICAL COSTS

Speaking of health, people can change their lives in ways that improve their physical condition. For example, they can quit smoking, stop eating junk food, and stay in shape. Now that they are hooked on bike riding, the Washingtons have become fitness enthusiasts of other outdoor activities, which makes their bodies stronger and reduces their medical bills.

UTILITIES

Benjamin Franklin, who once said, "A penny saved is a penny earned," would undoubtedly encourage people to save lots of pennies on utilities. By turning off lights and appliances when they are not in use, you can reduce electric bills. Lower your water bill by making sure your faucets have no drips. Do you have a cell phone? If so, you can cut your overall phone bill by eliminating your landline.

VACATION COSTS

A family vacation can cost an arm and a leg. The Washingtons have had several expensive vacations in Florida, California, and the Bahamas. In 2011, though, they are planning a "staycation"—a vacation close to home. To see where Abraham Lincoln lived and worked, they are visiting New Salem and Springfield in their home state of Illinois. It will be a fascinating and memorable family trip, yet it won't bust their budget.

CLOTHING

Like millions of other American families, the Washingtons have found ways to save at least a few hundred dollars a year on clothing. They buy store brands rather than pricier clothes with designer labels. They purchase some of their family's wardrobe at resale shops. Wearing hand-me-downs is another way to reduce the clothing budget.

COLLEGE

How can the Washingtons budget only $6,000 for a year of college? Several sources of aid are available to college students. There are government grants—monetary awards that don't have to be repaid. Scholarships—monetary awards that are often based on academic ability and achievement—also don't have to be repaid. Student loans, which must be repaid, are another source of money for college. In addition, many college students find jobs waiting tables, shelving library books, or working at a store in town to pay some of their expenses. With all these resources, Ernie and Rosalie only have to pay $6,000 of their own money for their daughter's year of college.

Students often get part-time jobs to help pay their college tuition—and to minimize student loans they must repay after graduation.

Can children—say, fifth or sixth graders—help their families spend less money? Absolutely! Here are a few simple ways that the Washingtons' children, Stephanie and Tony, save their family money:

- They turn off lights and the TV when they're not in use.
- They use no more water than necessary for baths and showers.
- They mow the lawn, rake leaves, and shovel snow at home; that way their parents don't have to hire someone to do these tasks.
- They don't nag their parents for costly items; if they've just got to have something, they earn money and buy it themselves.
- Tony helps his mom plant and tend their vegetable garden.
- Once a week, they prepare a meal for the family. By fixing dinner, they free up their parents to make more money at work.
- They help with household tasks such as setting the table, clearing dishes, and cleaning their rooms.
- Instead of always asking for a ride, Tony walks or rides his bike to nearby places (if it's okay with his folks).
- Tony wears his cousin's hand-me-downs.

One other thing. If you have questions about finances, ask your older relatives. They might never discuss money with you unless you bring up the subject. Listen to what they have to say. Spending money wisely and handling finances are among the great challenges facing Americans in the twenty-first century.

GLOSSARY

appliances — Home or business devices such as refrigerators, lamps, computers, TVs, and stoves.

automatic teller machine (ATM) — A device that allows people to withdraw money from their accounts without human help.

budget — A plan for spending money.

debt — A state of owing money to a business or an individual.

depression — A period of severe unemployment and reduced business activity.

down payment — Money paid for a house or other property at the time of purchase.

economists — Experts on money.

expenses — Money spent to do or buy something; costs.

finances — Money and other items of value.

financier — A person who raises money or who spends his or her money on major projects.

foreclosure — A process in which a bank takes over a home and forces the occupants to leave.

income — Money received for work done.

insurance — The business of providing protection against monetary loss; common types include automobile, homeowners, health, and life insurance.

interest — Extra money that must be paid in exchange for the privilege of borrowing money.

investments — Things in which money is used to buy something that will make more money. Examples of investments are stocks and bonds.

mortgage — A large loan for a house or other property.

overdraft — Money withdrawn from a bank account that is greater than the amount available.

property tax — A yearly fee charged by the local government where a property is located.

recession — A period of serious unemployment resulting from a business slump.

salaries — Money paid to someone at regular times (per week or per month) for work done.

taxes — Money paid to the government to support services such as education, transportation, and the military.

tenants — People who rent apartments or other types of property.

utilities — Services such as electricity, heat, water, telephone, cable TV, and Internet networks.

withdrawals — Money removed (withdrawn) from a salary or bank account.

FURTHER INFORMATION

BOOKS

Brancato, Robin F. *Money: Getting It, Using It, and Avoiding the Traps: The Ultimate Teen Guide*. Lanham, MD: The Scarecrow Press, 2007.

Deering, Kathryn R., editor. *Cash and Credit Information for Teens: Tips for a Successful Financial Life*. Detroit: Omnigraphics, 2005.

Hall, Margaret. *Banks*. Chicago: Heinemann Library, 2008.

——— *Credit Cards and Checks*. Chicago, Heinemann Library, 2008.

Holyoke, Nancy. *A Smart Girl's Guide to Money: How to Make It, Save It, and Spend It*. Middleton, WI: American Girl/Pleasant Company Publications, 2006.

Orr, Tamra. *Budgeting Tips for Kids*. Hockessin, DE: Mitchell Lane Publishers, 2009.

For a wealth of information about spending money from PBS Kids:

http://pbskids.org/itsmylife/money/spendingsmarts/index.html

For some basic facts about credit cards:

www.themint.org/kids/credit-card-facts.html

For information about the U.S. economy from *Scholastic News*:

www2.scholastic.com/browse/scholasticNews.
  jsp?FromBrowseMod=true&Ns=Pub_Date_
  Sort|1&CurrPage=scholasticNews.jsp&TopicValue=Scholastic%20
  News&ESP=SN/ib/20080922/eng/sn_art_top///cvr_logo/img///

For information about kids and money from North Dakota State
  University:

www.ext.nodak.edu/extnews/pipeline/k-goals.htm

BIBLIOGRAPHY

Economides, Steve, and Annette Economides. *America's Cheapest Family Gets You Right on the Money*. New York: Three Rivers Press, 2007.

Garner, Robert J., and others. *Ernst & Young's Personal Finance Planning Guide*. New York: John Wiley & Sons, 2000.

Hall, Alvin, with Karl Weber. *You and Your Money: It's More Than Just the Numbers*. New York: Atria Books, 2007.

Ivey, Allison. *The Geek's Guide to Personal Finance*. Birmingham, AL: Crane Hill Publishers, 2006.

Maranjian, Selena. *The Motley Fool Money Guide: Answers to Your Questions About Saving, Spending, and Investing*. Alexandria, VA: The Motley Fool, 2001.

Sander, Peter. *The Everything Personal Finance Book: Manage, Budget, Save, and Invest Your Money Wisely*. Avon, MA: Adams Media Corporation, 2003.

Savage, Terry. *The Savage Truth on Money*. New York: John Wiley & Sons, 1999.

Singletary, Michelle. *Spend Well, Live Rich: How to Get What You Want with the Money You Have*. New York: Ballantine, 2004.

INDEX

Dennis and Judy Fradin are the authors of more than 150 books. They co-author many of their books, but in some cases Dennis writes the text and Judy obtains the pictures. The Fradins first became known for their fifty-two-book series about the states, *From Sea to Shining Sea*, which they did for Children's Press. Their first series for Marshall Cavendish Benchmark was *Turning Points in U.S. History*.

In recent years the Fradins have written many award-winning books about the Underground Railroad, early American history, and great but underappreciated women. Their Clarion book *The Power of One: Daisy Bates and the Little Rock Nine* was named a Golden Kite Honor Book. Another of their Clarion books, *Jane Addams: Champion of Democracy* won the Society of Midland Authors Best Children's Nonfiction Book of the Year Award.

Currently the Fradins are working on several projects, including a picture book about a slave escape for Walker and a book on *Tornadoes* for National Geographic Children's Books. In addition, Dennis is writing the text and Judy is obtaining the pictures for *Kids Who Overcame*, a book about young people who overcame handicaps to achieve something noteworthy.

The Fradins have three grown children and six grandchildren. In their free time, Judy is a passionate gardener with a special love for dahlias, and Dennis is an amateur astronomer and huge baseball fan.